Bonjour La Poésie

Aisha Idris Suleman

BookLeaf Publishing

India | USA | UK

Presentation by *BookLeaf Publishing*

Web: www.bookleafpub.com

E-mail: info@bookleafpub.com

ISBN: 9789357214988

First edition 2022

This time, I want to dedicate this book to all my wonderful readers and supporters around the world. Whatever your age, ethnicity, gender, sexuality or religion, you all truly encouraged me to fly towards my dreams. Let's soar!

ACKNOWLEDGEMENT

I want to express my special thanks of gratitude to all my lovely readers, supporters, fans, friends, family and the wider community, who have always stood by me in my writing journey and have made my dream of becoming an author come true. I would also like to thank my late father, who taught me to follow my dreams and never give up, as well as my lucky son, who motivates me every single day.

Most of all, I want to thank BookLeaf Publishing yet again for giving me the golden opportunity to showcase my talent to the world and publishing my fourth book!

PREFACE

This book of poetry consists of poems relating to various themes, which have been written over the last two years. I want my audience to understand that poetry is not dead and that anyone can be a poet, as you do not need to be experienced in order to write. I see poetry as a form of therapy, where you can easily write what you are feeling from the inside. It is a way of expressing how you feel about certain things, whether it is related to your life or the outside world. As you read through my poems in this book, you will notice how I have put my entire heart and soul to them, which helps to capture and communicate a message. No two poems will ever be the same and each one will express different emotions.

This book of poetry is unique, compared to my previous books, as my main message is that poetry is for all us and that this can be used as a bridge to connection. Poetry remains a niche market, and mainly attracts a small number of the population. This is the reason why I have written this book, so I can give my audience around the world a glimpse of what poetry actually is and how we all have the power to write our own poetry and talk about important issues that all human beings care about, such as love, loss, inspiration, motivation and many others. I have come across many people from different walks of life that have expressed how my poems are a voice to communities and how many mindsets have changed the way they view life, which is a very positive thing to hear!

So together, let us say Bonjour La Poésie, and let our minds speak for itself!

The Feeling Of Love

The feeling of love

Like the blue sky above

So great and touching

With some kissing and hugging

The soul feeling amused

Two hearts firmly fused

What a beautiful sensation

Without any exaggeration

As if surrounded by flowers

The feeling goes beyond twenty four hours

One that has no full stop

Two bodies that just want to hop

Filling life with laughter and joy

A strong bond which nobody can destroy!

The Breeze

The beautiful breeze

Tall green trees

Fluffy white clouds

Far from the crowds

Eyes deeply closed

Just want to be exposed

To the gentle wind

Oh what a cute hind

The lovely blue sky

Holding my head up high

Walking on the green grass

Watching the birds fly pass

What an exquisite sensation

Mood and weather, such a good combination

Want to feel this breeze forever

Time to embark on another venture!

Summer

The beauty of summer

The feeling of a stunner

Barbeques and salads

Hearing sweet ballads

Going to beaches

Munching on peaches

Enjoying the glorious sun

Without hesitation, only fun

Wearing outfits and flip-fops

Even loose tees or tops

All geared for the season

That is just one good reason

Get your bags and tickets ready

Time to dance and shake like jelly!

People With Hearts

The world is full of different people

Some at home, others on the steeple

A few that shows care and appreciation

While others paint their true image with decoration

No two people will ever be the same

Some with pure hearts, others just playing a game

Making it difficult to trust and believe

Since nowadays it is all about lies and deceives

Being nice has become a crime

Similar to thick windows covered in grime

As people can easily back stab you

Even if your intentions are clear and true!

Lover

Oh my sweet lover

Just let me discover

The beauty in your eyes

Without any games or lies

A gentle stroke on the arm

What a beautiful charm

Though we are far apart

Technology brings together our hearts

Enjoying every moment and feeling

Like stars pouring from the ceiling

A lost moon seems to have been found

Feet stuck to the solid ground

Lips chanting your lovely name

Without any fear or shame

Let this emotion unfold gradually

And watch us walk through this experience
magically!

Love Games

You are such a beauty

Which I gaze like my duty

Perfection top to bottom

Always glowing, whether summer or autumn

Something about you I admire

My soul is always lighting up with fire

Expressed to you in many forms

So loudly, like the sound of storms

I see something similar in your eyes

Let us be playful and forget the lies

Why be hard on ourselves?

And be hidden like books on shelves

Keep it low and private

But let our hearts drive it

I name it love games

That runs down our veins!

Lost In Paradise

Let's get lost in paradise

Where the river streams flow and the air smells nice

No looking back and forth

Standing on top of the hills up north

Watching the beautiful white clouds

No sound of traffic or crowds

Such a lovely image to capture

Maybe one part of our chapter

The taste of delicious fruits

All dressed in outfits and suits

The party has just begun

With non-stop dancing and fun

Is this the reality or a dream?

Try not to wake me up or scream

Let the snow of petals brush against my skin

Until I am wide awake with a grin!

Happy Days

Let the happy days kick in

Throw the past in the bin

It may have taught you a lesson

But you are still in the right direction

No need to look back

Relax and remain on track

There is so much to look forward to

Maybe travelling or visiting the zoo

Just let the magic unfold gradually

Good days come naturally

Just be you and stay patient

And focus on the nascent!

Every Little Counts

Every little counts

So just announce

Small steps daily

Makes a difference greatly

Keep the motivation going

Like water gradually flowing

Just don't ever give up

Clutch that miracle filled inside the cup

Let go of the fear

And just happily appear

In every step of life

Sometimes peace, sometimes strife

So celebrate every milestone

Either with everyone or alone

Push yourself to the best of your abilities

Regardless of any insecurities or disabilities!

The Wind

The sound of wind

The lights are dimmed

Watch the trees swaying side by side

Similar to an unpredictable tide

Let this wind erase your pain

Without leaving any harsh stains

The breeze brushing against your skin

Closing your eyes knowing you can win

Feeling the cold touch your body

Gazing at the clouds, since it isn't foggy

Such a beautiful feeling inside out

Don't want it to end without any doubt

So let the wind release your inner soul

Don't look around, just let it control

Forgetting what is going on around you

Let the wind help you discover a world you
never knew!

The Parcel Courier

When he knocks on the door
It feels nothing like before
He gazes into my eyes
Making my beautiful soul rise

He greets me with a smile
Standing on the doorstep for a while
Probably wants to utter some words
Similar to flocking and hungry birds

He seems like a charm
That can be of no harm
Though he is a stranger
I cannot disregard the danger

He does not feel like leaving
Staring at my long hair swerving
He grins as I give him chocolates
Taking his hands out of his pockets

He is like fizzy lemonade
Freshens me in leafy glade
I don't know who he is
Probably time to take his quiz!

That Time Of Season – Winter

Here comes that time of season
That always has a valid reason
Wrapping up in the cosy duvet
Similar to robbing the Goulet

Wearing those thick and warm socks
That feels like it is stuffed with rocks
Turning the heating on day and night
And watching the striking darkness, no light

Having warm drinks and soup
To avoid nasty aches and croup
Popping on the jacket and gloves
Pretending these are the things she loves

Wrapping gifts, eager to see friends
These habits of hers has no ends
Spreading laughter, love and joy
And avoiding all forms of decoy

'Tis the season to be cheery
No need to feel so weary
Let the snow fall and enter
It is that beautiful season of Winter!

Festival Of Lights

Here comes the festival of lights
The one that makes the year bright
Gathering, eating and praying together
Similar to the shining sapphire weather

Diwali is the time for celebrations
No need to send out specific invitations
The entire nation can join in
Regardless of race, ethnicity and skin

Let us all celebrate Diwali together
And remain as one forever
Though the lockdown has struck hard
Be safe and enjoy it in your backyard!

Don't Be My Guest Covid

You have hit us all so hard
My heart feels deeply scarred
When are you going to let us go?
You have already given us a big blow

Many lives have been lost
But how would you understand the cost?
You just want to take take take
And continue spreading the damn outbreak

Life has become so boring and dull
It has traumatised my inner skull
Let us live our lives to the fullest
As we have been hit with a thousand bullets

What is it you want from us?
You are silent that we cannot discuss
Snatching such innocent people
Making us preach in front of the steeple

Don't be my guest you nasty Covid
Or more lives will be snatched, God forbid
You killed my best friend, my father
For whom there was no funeral or gather!

Lockdown Blues

Once again we feel blue
 Without having a clue
 When life will go back to normal
 Without getting too formal

The lockdown has begun
There is no place to run
I can only sense misery
That is causing a lot of injury

We need to make the most of it
To ensure we don't fully quit
Maybe learn a new skill
Rather than just sitting still

Life does not end here
Wriggle to the front and rear
The good times will come
So don't be so glum

I am here to spread laughter
Join me either before or after
I won't let lockdown blues win
Let the fight begin!

My Adorable Darling

My adorable darling
 You are my prince charming
 I think of you night and morning
 Even when I am busy or yawning!

My adorable darling
You are my exotic starling
My heart chants your exquisite name
Without any regret or shame!

My adorable darling
Tonight there will be no quarrelling
Because your eyes make me feel warm
Despite the rain, thunder and storm!

My adorable darling
You look endearing whilst snarling
We are two bodies and one soul
Which will remain our everlasting goal!

There are times when we smile
There are times when we cry
But you will remain my adorable darling
Until the day we die!

The One I Love

My prince charming
 You are my night and morning
 I feel your presence all day
 Even when we are miles away

My enchanting man
 I have become your greatest fan
 Your eyes make me feel warm
 Despite the gloomy storm

My caring honey
 At times you can be so funny
 My soul chants your nice name
 Without any remorse or shame

My one and only love
 You are always foremost and above
 Our two bodies and one soul
 Will remain our eternal goal!

Holidays

The holidays are finally here
Dance to the front, dance to the rear
Let the soul unwind and undo
Yet there is so much to get through

Countdown for Christmas has begun
But nothing much can be done
Back into lockdown, now tier four
No more guests knocking at the door

Last minute plans have to change
The whole process feels boring and strange
Lives must be saved, especially of the
vulnerable
Since Covid is so stubborn and unstoppable

Still need to make the most of the holidays
Need to think of a million different ways
Hoping next year will be happy and normal
Without any strict rules or being formal!

Full Lockdown Again

Here comes the full lockdown yet again
How much more is Covid going to cause pain?
Taking away so many innocent lives
It is worse than the sharp kitchen knives

Many people feeling depressed and isolated
What an awful scenario Covid has created
Not able to do the things that we all enjoy
We must abide by the governments' deploy

Stay at home and protect each other
Whether it is your mother, sister or brother
Utilise your time at home wisely
And keep in touch carefree and kindly

Don't let the lockdown beat you
Or make you feel sad and blue
Do the things you enjoy, maybe a new hobby
Probably painting, DIY or moving your body

Despite the tough times we are facing
And the restrictions we are chasing
All this will sooner or later be over
And the view of life will be much sober!

Hate Song

I hate you like a hate song
 Your thinking is so wrong
 You can avoid and block
 Twenty-four-seven around the clock

You are magical and unique
I keep hitting repeat-peat-peat
You play through my mind
So gentle and peaceful I find

No words can describe you
You do it, but what is it you do?
Is it the style or dazzling flare?
Definitely something beyond compare

Who cares about life tags or labels?
Let us explore like mixed cables
What is it that you are scared about?
You know you want to without any doubt!

Aim High

As we enter the New Year
Forget all your worries and fear
Set yourself worthy goals
That may revive your souls

Don't linger on the past
Life is going extremely fast
Live up each and every dream
Rise and shine with every morning's beam

Show the world what you are capable of
Not forgetting to still spread peace and love
Reach for the sky and aim as high as you can
Grasp a pen and paper and make a good plan

So experience every moment, big or small
Don't let any barriers give you a haul
Never give up and show that courage
Either sharply or with gentle steerage!